Captain John Smith
of Willoughby and
the founding of America

by

John Haden and the Pupils of
Willoughby and Partney Schools

ISBN No: 1.903172.46.2

Publishers: Barny Books
                 Hough on the Hill,
                 Grantham,
                 Lincolnshire
                 NG32 2BB

                 Tel: 01400 250246

Foreword

Four hundred years ago, Guy Fawkes and his Catholic friends were plotting to blow up King James when he opened Parliament. Nearby, in the City of London, four rich and influential men were planning how best to persuade the same King James to grant them exclusive rights to the settlement of that part of the North American coast called Virginia. When the Gunpowder Plot was discovered, it was Fawkes and the plotters who died, executed as traitors. King James survived and the leaders of the Virginia Company were granted their Charter. They raised money and recruited settlers for what was essentially a business venture. Just before Christmas 1606, three small ships sailed for Virginia. Amongst the men on board was a soldier and farmer's son from Lincolnshire, John Smith of Willoughby.

He was only twenty six and had already survived wars in Holland and Hungary. He had travelled over much of Europe and acquired at least the trappings of a gentleman. Within two years of arriving in Virginia, he became the leader of the Jamestown colony, saving it from the failure that had ended so many earlier English attempts to establish settlements in North America. If you visit Jamestown today, the only statues on the shore are those of Captain John Smith and the American Indian Princess, Pocahontas, who twice saved his life.

This short book has been written and illustrated with the help of pupils and their Headteachers from two village schools which have links with his early life, St Helena's Church of England Primary School, Willoughby, and Partney Church of England VA Primary School. We hope that our account of the early life of Captain John Smith, President of Virginia, also helps to celebrate the 400th anniversary of the founding of Jamestown and the start of the American dream.

The Lincolnshire area as it is today

Born in Willoughby

John Smith was born in the small Lincolnshire village of Willoughby, which lies in the east of the County, where the Lincolnshire Wolds meet the flat land which runs out to the North Sea coast. From the top of the Wolds, you can see the great towers of Lincoln's Cathedral on the western horizon, and the square brick keep of Tattershall Castle rising up from the valley of the River Bain. Willoughby is near the market towns of Alford, Spilsby and Louth, all places which played a part in John Smith's early life.

On January 9th 1580, a farmer called George Smith and his wife Alice brought their first-born son to be baptised in Willoughby's St Helena's Church. They named him John.

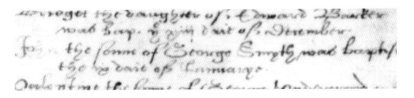

Record of John Smith's baptism from the Register of St Helen's Church, Willoughby

 The stone baptismal font still stands by the south door of the church and a fine set of stained glass windows celebrates the story of John Smith's life and the early history of Virginia.

Sir Peregrine Bertie had just become Lord Willoughby de Eresby and Lord of the Manor of the village of Willoughby. He had a large house near Spilsby and a home at Grimsthorpe Castle in the south of the County. John's father rented a farm of over 100 acres from Lord Willoughby. He also owned seven acres in the village of Great Carlton and three plots in the street called Westgate in the town of Louth.

St Helena's Church, Willoughby

One of the windows
illustrating the baptism
of John Smith

George Smith could not call himself a gentleman as he
owned too little land and had no coat of arms. But he was
much better off than most of his neighbours; a yoeman
farmer with a comfortable house of five rooms, somewhere
in Willoughby village.

We know from George Smith's will that this house had solid oak beds, chairs and tables, painted cloth hangings to decorate the walls of his hall and brass and pewter plates and jugs on his table. He had cattle in his fields and hay in his barns. It was a peaceful and relatively prosperous farming household. The Smiths made their own butter and cheese, grew their own wheat for bread and barley for brewing beer. They would have used wool from their sheep for spinning and weaving and their own oxen for ploughing the land. George Smith bred horses, the best of these were good enough to offer Lord Willoughby as a gift from a loyal and respectful tenant.

Today's rare breeds which are the descendents of Old English Long-horn cattle and Lincolnshire Longwool sheep

No-one really knows where in Willoughby the Smith's farm was sited. There are no surviving Tudor houses and no records left from that time. The most likely place is now called Covell's Farm, at the end of School Lane. This two storey brick private house has clues which could link it to a humbler beginning. The ground floor windows are small and square and an upper floor has been added. There could have been an earlier single storey cottage made of 'mud and stud' under the brick work, similar to the cottages which still exist in other villages in their original form. Archaeologists working in America have found that the earliest houses built there by the English were of 'mud and stud' construction, typical of the houses built by farming families in the part of Lincolnshire in which John Smith was born.

Covell's Farm in Willoughby

Mud and Stud building in Billinghay

Building a mud and stud house.

'The men would cut down small trees from the hedgerow to make a framework. To make the walls, they had to attach strips of wood into the frame and cover them over with clay or mud which had been 'puddled', by digging a pit and trampling the clay and water with bare feet. The mud plaster would stick to the wood to make the walls come to life and make the house insulated to keep warm. More mud was plastered on the walls, covering over the timber frame. The roof was thatched and the earth floor sealed with ox blood. The chimney was also a vital aspect of houses back then, as they did not have electricity nor did they have radiators. The only heat supply was a fire, usually located in the centre of the house. Their furniture was very different from ours, hand-crafted out of timber by a local carpenter. The carpenters never used to charge very much as there were many carpenters around at the time. (Joshua W.)

All the old 'mud and stud' houses in Willoughby village have now been bricked up or taken down but there are still many left in nearby villages. The old Post Office in Billinghay and the Royal Oak public house in Mareham le Fen, are good examples.

George Smith's family came from Lancashire in the northwest of England. His wife, Alice, came from Yorkshire, north of the Humber. Most people in the Tudor period stayed in the area where their families had lived for generations. The villagers of Willoughby must have thought of the Smiths as outsiders. John Smith would have felt different, the son of a yeoman, somewhere between the poorer farming families of the village and the leading

Lincolnshire gentlemen, the Willoughbys of Grimsthorpe Castle and the Clintons of Tattershall.

The Royal Oak public house in Mareham le Fen, a mud and stud structure claiming to date from the 15th Century

In their remote corner of rural England, it is doubtful whether George and Alice Smith would have been aware of the major events in the world beyond their village in the decade after John's birth. In 1580, the two great European powers, Spain and Portugal were united under Philip of Spain when the King of Portugal died without an heir. This made the Spanish the masters not only of their vast empire in the Americas but also of the rich trading routes which the Portuguese had developed around Africa to India and as far as the coast of China.

The Spanish in America

In September of 1580, Sir Francis Drake sailed the Golden Hind back to Plymouth in England after his three year voyage right round the world. He brought back a fabulous cargo of gold and silver, the product of his attacks on Spanish ships. Drake presented a major share of this bullion to the grateful Queen Elizabeth I.

Collage of Elizabeth I by the pupils of Studio 3, Willoughby School

Queen Elizabeth I had actively encouraged her sea-captains to plunder the Spanish, calling them 'privateers', although to the Spanish, they were 'pirates'. Many of the English captains grew rich as they intercepted cargoes of gold and silver from the conquered empires of the Aztecs of Mexico and the Incas of Peru. With the gold came new foods; tomatoes, peppers, maize, potatoes and sweet potatoes, avocados, pineapples and chocolate. Brightly coloured parrots, captive Carib Indians and Mexican jugglers were seen in Europe for the first time at the court of the Spanish King. With gold from the Americas, and control of the trade in spices and silks from the East, Spain became the most powerful nation in Europe. Spain was also the champion of the Roman Catholic Church, with a hatred of the Protestant English and their heretic Queen.

But if the Spanish could find gold in the Americas and trade with the East, so could the English, or so they believed. In 1487, not long after Columbus' first voyage to the Americas, Henry Cabot sailed an English ship across the north Atlantic, trying to find a way through to China around the north of the continent. He landed on the island which he called Newfoundland, but there was no route through the ice to China. His sailors brought back stories of strange animals they had seen, great white bears on the ice and whales in the freezing water with single horns like unicorns.

The French too explored the North American coast and established their first settlements, the start of French-speaking Canada. They also had a small French settlement just north of the Spanish in Florida, but the ruthless Spanish wiped this out. Throughout the 16th century, fishermen from Portugal, France, Spain and England made their fortunes by bringing back dried cod from the rich fishing grounds of the north east coast. Cod still makes up a national dish in Portugal today. But it was the hope of finding either gold and/or a route through the new continent to the Pacific which drove explorers further north and further inland. In the 1570's, Martin Frobisher from Yorkshire sailed three times to the frozen coast of Labrador, to bring back samples and even cargoes of rock which looked like gold. But to the amusement of Spanish spies in London, the rock turned out to be 'fool's gold', a worthless ore of iron.

English claims

There was just one part of the American coast north of the Spanish in Florida and south of the French in Canada which no-one from Europe had claimed. Queen Elizabeth gave an English sailor, Sir Humphrey Gilbert, permission to try to take over this part of the American shore. He was told to *'search, find out and view such remote, heathen and barbarous lands, countries and territories, not actually possessed of any Christian Prince or people, and the same to have, hold, occupy and enjoy to him, his heirs and assigns for ever'.* The Spanish were angry at this attempt to grab part of *their* continent and of course the people who already lived there, the Native American peoples were not consulted. Many had already died from the devastating 'gift' of infection by measles and smallpox and other European diseases against which they had no resistance.

Gilbert's ships did reach Newfoundland, but they found that Cabot's sailors had been right. There was no way through to China and it was far too cold for English gentlemen to want to stay there. On their voyage home, Gilbert's ship, the 'Squirrel' sank in a storm, with Sir Humphrey sitting on the deck, calmly reading a book. Queen Elizabeth commented that Humphrey Gilbert 'was not of good hap by sea'.

When Gilbert died the Queen's agreement for exploration and settlement was transferred to his half-brother Walter Raleigh. He was Elizabeth's favourite, rich from the licences the Queen gave him. She made him 'Sir Walter', and the Captain of her personal Guard. When Sir Walter wanted to name the new lands which he hoped to discover in America, Virginia, in honour of the Virgin Queen, she graciously agreed.

Failure at Roanoke

Raleigh chose Roanoke Island, tucked away behind the Outer Banks of what is now North Carolina, for his new settlement but he never went there himself. Three times between 1584 and 1587, he sent ships and men to set up a colony, but each time they failed. Roanoke was a good place for English ships to hide from the eyes of the Spanish and a useful base from which to attack their ships, but it was a bad choice for a colony. The soil was sandy and not good for growing English crops. The coast was very dangerous; even today, it is called the 'graveyard of the Atlantic'. Hurricanes sweep in from the southwest in the summer, and, in winter, northeast gales blow over the sandbanks. On the landward side, an area still called the Great Dismal Swamp was very difficult to cross, the home of bears and alligators.

The South Carolina Outer Banks which shelter Roanoke Island

Roanoke Island was, however, the first English colony in Virginia to survive for any length of time. When the first history of Virginia was written many years later by John Smith, his map of 'Ould Virginia' shows Roanoke Island. But the swamps inland are shown with other settlements and fertile farmland, all products of his imagination. There is even an area 'Alice Smith's Field' in honour of his mother.

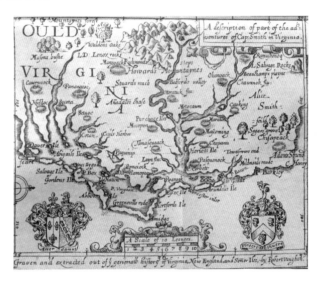

Smith's map of 'Ould Virginia'

The Roanoke colony could only survive by being supplied by ships from England, three thousands miles away across the Atlantic. That became impossible in 1588, when every English ship was needed to defend England against invasion. King Philip of Spain sent a huge fleet, the Spanish Armada, sweeping up the Channel to ferry the Spanish army in the Low Countries across the Dover Straits to invade England. The Spanish planned to remove Elizabeth and return England to the Catholic faith. Drake, Frobisher, Raleigh, and all Elizabeth's Captains attacked the Spanish, but it was the weather that proved decisive, blowing the Spanish ships towards the Channels' southern shore.

King Philip II of Spain by Studio 3

The Spanish Armada and the English fleet off Calais on 6 August 1588, shown in Pine's engraving from the House of Lords' tapestries.

On board ship fighting the Spanish Armada, July 29th 1588

'The huge Spanish fleet is lying at anchor close to the shore. They have fallen back under the firing of our guns but there are still enough of them to defeat us! All of the eight fire ships have been sent out but only five Spanish ships have been destroyed, one of them crashed and sank as she was trying to escape. The sea is full of smoke and gun fire, the sounds of broken wood, twisted metal, firing cannons and men screaming as their ships are sinking, on fire or falling to pieces.

I kept on firing although I hought that we were all going to die. All of a sudden my cannon kicked and exploded furiously, as thick black smoke spread across the ship. My leg cracked on the face of the cannon, maybe it's broken and badly burnt. Pain throbbed in and out of my leg. My Uncle Edward's voice faded and everything was ruined as our foremast started to catch fire. We're surely going to sink and die. At a snail's pace I started to crawl away from the cannon and on to the main deck, where men lay dead under splintered wood.' (Theo H. and Adam R.)

The Spanish ships struggled to escape into the North Sea and sail right round the coasts of Scotland and Ireland, to get back to Spain. Without their anchors, many were driven onto the rocky shore and wrecked. England was saved, but by the time it was possible to send supplies to Roanoke again, all trace of Raleigh's Virginian colony had disappeared. Almost a hundred years after Columbus had established Spanish settlements in the Americas, the English had still failed to occupy any part of the North American shore.

Going to school

John Smith was eight when the Armada sailed. He must have seen the great beacon fires that carried the good news of Elizabeth's victory all round England. He would also have been kept busy by the rigorous demands of the Tudor school system. Boys and girls were first sent to local 'petty schools', to learn to read and write. They used 'horn books' to learn to read, single sheets showing the Alphabet or the Lord's Prayer, attached to a wooden board and covered with a layer of transparent cow horn to keep the page clean from grubby fingers. For writing, they used the sharpened point of a goose feather or quill, softened with spit and dipped in thick black ink, which must have made the first steps in the tricky skill of forming letters a very messy business.

Richer families could afford to send their sons to the nearest grammar school as soon as they could read and write. Many children did not go to school at all because their families needed the help of their children to care for younger children, to guard the sheep or weed the garden.

The south porch of St Wilfrid's Church, Alford,
with the school room above

For John Smith, the nearest school was in Alford, where, in 1575, the Queen had allowed the people to call their school, Queen Elizabeth's Grammar School. The school was at first held in the parish Church of St Wilfrid's, in a small room above the south porch, although it moved to a new building at about the time that John Smith was there. Boys brought their own candles for the dark mornings and evenings and had to provide their own quill pens and knives to sharpen them. (We still call small pocket-knives, 'pen-knives'.) Holidays were short, at Christmas, Easter and Whitsun. There was no long summer break but there were all the Saints Days, Holy Days, which we call 'holidays'!

Following in John Smith's footsteps to school

'It was an awful day, wet, windy and freezing, when we set out from St Helena's C of E Primary School, to find out what it was like to be him as a small boy walking to school from Willoughby to Alford. So Ashley, Harry, Theo, Jonathan, Becky, Chloe, Thomas and Emily walked over three miles across the muddy fields. When we arrived at Alford Church, Mrs Sharpe told us all about the old school room called the "parvis room", up a winding stone staircase in the church porch. We think that they called it that because 'parva' means small in Latin. It was only 3.6m by 3.7m, so the school must have been very small. Mr Weaver told us what teachers taught in those days and what it must have been like to walk to school in pitch black in the winter. We were absolutely soaked by the time we arrived at Alford but we survived the worst. Thank Étienne Lenoir who invented the car, which takes us dry to school nowadays!' (Emily B.)

Going up to the Parvis Room, Alford Parish Church

Latin formed the basis of most lessons, boys learning long passages by heart from books such as Aesop's Fables. Those who were slower to learn were encouraged by frequent beatings. Grammar schools used a Latin book written by the Master of St Paul's School in London which so impressed Henry VIII that he ordered that it be used in all schools. It continued in use for about three hundred years!

Life at school
'Most days, I have to run to school. When I get to school, I get out my quill and start writing. I also have to learn my Latin verbs, Amo, Amas, Amat, and we have to learn the Lord's Prayer, in Latin of course!

I get the birch at school for making ink blotches on my work. "It was a mistake, Sir." "John Smith, you know we don't allow mistakes in this school. Bend over, boy!" I bend over. "Stand still boy." WHACK! "AAAH!" WHACK! "AAAH!" WHACK! "AAAH!" I scream in agony. I can still feel the pain as I try to sit down to write the rest of my work.' If only I could leave school and go to sea and become 'Captayne John Smith'. (Harriet H and Hannah M.)

There was not much history or geography, very little mathematics apart from simple adding and subtracting and no sport. On Thursdays, school ended early so that boys could practise archery, by order of Henry VIII. Willoughby has some ancient yew trees, whose branches could be cut for making long bows, which grow in the churchyard so that the villagers' cattle did not eat the poisonous berries. Even on Sundays, boys would not be free to play games on the town or village green. If they wanted to play a new game called 'foot-ball' which was thought to be very dangerous, they had to attend church first.

Children's games, from a Tudor woodcut

Schoolboys were taught to be polite and respectful to their parents, to behave well and to accept the main beliefs of the Protestant Church of England. When John Smith first joined the Alford School, the Rev Francis Marbury was well established as the schoolmaster. He had studied at Cambridge University, then a centre of Puritan teaching.

Marbury was outspoken and critical of the church authorities. Even before coming to Alford, he had been in trouble with the Bishops and had served a prison sentence for saying that Bishops were unfit for their calling. He was described by his accusers as a 'proud Puritan knave'.

John Smith spent four years as Marbury's pupil in the Alford school, learning from him the Puritan way of life. Through all his later adventures, John Smith followed this way. He never swore, never drank strong liquor or smoked tobacco, all very unusual for a man who became a tough soldier. When John was eleven, Francis Marbuy's outspoken criticism of the church finally provoked the Bishop into dismissing him from his post as schoolmaster and preacher and confining him to a form of house arrest in Alford. He devoted his time to educating his own family, especially his daughters who had no opportunity of going to school. One of these girls, Anne, grew up to be Mrs Anne Hutchinson, taking her family to New England in the 1630s and causing a great deal of trouble in the new colony there. She was known as the 'troubler of Zion'.

Moving school to Louth

Shortly after Marbury had been replaced at Alford, John Smith 'decided to sell his satchel and his books and run away to sea'.

Planning to escape
'At the table, I was chewing on the strange concoction my mother had salvaged from last night's meal when I noticed the list of jobs on the slate board I had to do before school:

*feed the animals, help around the house, collect the eggs, separate the grain. I sighed a solemn sigh and reluctantly poked around my pewter plate. When was I to sail the world? When was I to find a new and exotic landscape? Not now, that was for certain. I grabbed my bag, ignoring the list of jobs on the board and set off half-heartedly to school. The cold November morning yawned through the trees in a weary melancholy sort of way and the path seemed to turn over in its sleep, drawing me in to its careless slumber. The school was in my view now. I tried to shake it out of my head but the thought kept creeping back to my mind, I couldn't stand it any longer. I was sick and tired of this routine. I had to escape, I **had** to run away!' (Theo H.)*

John Smith
flailing corn
By Chloe A.

He did not get far. His father sent him back to school, not in Alford but to the larger market town of Louth, about ten miles to the north. Louth Grammar School already had a strong reputation, as the Lincolnshire saying puts it: 'Sleaford for sleep, Boston for business, Horncastle for horses, Louth for learning'. John Smith's father owned property in Westgate in Louth and it is likely that John would have stayed there, rather than travel daily from home in Willoughby. Moving school is a major upheaval in any child's life. At the age of twelve, John Smith must have found the rough world of a Tudor schoolboy a good preparation for survival in later life.

Parish Church of St James in Westgate, Louth

The Louth School had started in the Parish Church of St James, where the Vicar had been involved in the Lincolnshire rebellion in 1536 against Henry VIII when the King decided to close all the monasteries, including the rich Abbey at Louth Park. When the King's men came to the town, the people were worried that their beautiful parish church might also be affected. They armed themselves with farming tools and marched to Lincoln with men from other towns joining them along the way. But the rebellion quickly collapsed when the King threatened them with punishment as traitors. Most of the rebels escaped but the Vicar of Louth was executed with the other leaders by being hung, drawn and quartered in London. As always, the King had the last word:

'How presumptuous then are ye, the rude commons of one shire, and that one of the most brute and beastly of the whole realm, and one of the least experience, to find fault with your prince.'

King Edward VI Grammar School on Schoolhouse Lane, Louth

The school was re-founded by King Edward VI and moved from the old parish church, to a new site on a street called Schoolhouse Lane, just off Westgate. There, the school flourished in a thatched mud and stud building which survived for over two hundred years. Part of the school is still on this same site, with a large school-room like the room in which John Smith had all his lessons. Although there are no school records which include John Smith, his time at the school is celebrated by a bust by Lord Baden Powell in this building and a mural painting in the school's Edward Street Hall. The School also has a collection of school books which date from this Tudor period including a Latin text published in the year of Smith's birth and a 'nomenclature' which gives Tudor medical terms in four languages, Latin, Greek, French and English!

Bust of Captain John Smith
by Lord Baden Powell

1580 edition of a school text
Cicero's speeches

Vomitus, *Celfo*, *ReieƈTio eorum que in ventriculi ſpatio conti-nentur.ἐμετὸς.* Vomiſſement. **Uomiting : perbreaking : ſpewing: caſting of the gorge.**

Nauſea, *Plin. Inane vomendi de-ſiderium.ναυτία.*Appetit de vo-mir. **A deſire to bomit, but no bomit: when one feeleth in him ſelfe offers to bomit, but can not caſt.**

The difference bewtween 'being sick' and 'feeling sick' from a Tudor 'Nomenclature'

The old badge of Louth School gives a good idea of what the school was like when John Smith joined, with the master thrashing a boy across his knee. All the teaching and learning was in Latin. John will have heard the stories in Latin which William Shakespeare learnt in his grammar school at Stratford on Avon and used in his plays. John will have also become fluent in spoken Latin. Written English at that time had no agreed system of spelling, so his reputation as a poor speller is a little unfair.

Louth was a busy market town with many ale-houses. The Weatsheaf and the Old White Swann both started in the early 17th century and still serve 'good honest ales' to thirsty farmers coming in to the markets three days a week.

Two pubs in Louth claiming to be in business in the 17th Century

The Wheatsheaf (1625)

The Olde White Swan (1612)

Farming disaster

William Shakespeare by Emily B.

In the 1590's, a sequence of bad summers and disastrous harvests inspired Shakespeare to put these words into the mouth of the boy playing Titania in 'A Midsummer Night's Dream'.

Contagious fogs; which falling in the land,
Hath every pelting river made so proud
That they have overborne their continents.
The ox hath therefore stretch'd his yoke in vain,
The ploughman lost his sweat, and the green corn
Hath rotted ere his youth attain'd a beard;
The fold stands empty in the drowned field,
The crows are fatted with the murrion flock;
The nine men's morris is filled up with mud,
And the quaint mazes in the wanton green,
For lack of tread, are indistinguishable.'

Or as a twenty first century pupil put it:

'It's chucking it down again. It has been raining all summer and all day so I can't do anything outside. The clouds are black and full of rain. In my bedroom, I was watching TV and on the news it said that the rivers were overflowing their banks. The farmers' tractors were stuck in the muddy fields. The crops were all rotting in the wet fields and the sheep got soaked. All the football matches had been cancelled, so Dad was bored all evening!   (Gemma T.)

John Smith left King Edward VI Grammar School in 1595. It was not a good time to start life as a tenant farmer and his father decided to send him away again, finding him a place as an apprentice to the merchant, Thomas Sendall, in the busy port of King's Lynn, on the Norfolk side of the great bay of the Wash. Sendall was already well established, a trader in wool and wine, a leading citizen and Mayor of the town. The merchants of Kings Lynn were part of the Hanseatic League, a trading organisation which linked them with the powerful merchants of German cities across the North Sea. Through the League, they controlled most of the trade in Northern Europe and made the merchants of King's

Lynn very rich. Sendall's house is thought to be the building now known as the Tudor Rose in St Nicholas Street.

The Green Quay on the banks of the Ouse, King's Lynn

The Tudor Rose Hotel, King's Lynn

John Smith had dreamed of such an opportunity, to go to sea, visit other lands and have what he called 'brave adventures'. But that was not what Sendall had in mind for him. As a merchant's apprentice, Smith was bound by agreement to serve for seven years before being free to set up on his own. In the streets and ale houses of King's Lynn, he was surrounded by stories of travel and trade, from the sea captains and sailors who had travelled all over Europe. But John was put to work in Sendell's counting house and stores, learning to enter lists of goods in ledgers and to check orders to be sent across the North Sea.

He lasted just one year of this apprenticeship, when he heard that his father had died. John used this news as an excuse to break his agreement and leave his master's service without permission. He 'never saw his master in eight years after', getting back to Willoughby in time for the reading of his father's will. This gave the best of George's two-year old colts to Lord Willoughby, the owner of the farm, together with the advice to John to honour and love his Lordship. John's mother, Alice got the tenancy of the farm and the best bed, on condition that she did not marry again. When she did marry again, very quickly, the farm and the bed came to John.

John also inherited the seven acres of land in Great Carlton. His brother Francis got the property in Westgate, Louth. All the other items were to be divided equally between the brothers, with George Smith's friend, George Metham, appointed guardian to the three children.

Now that he was free from his parents and his indentures, John Smith could decide his own future. He could have stayed in Willoughby and worked the farm as his father had done. But having attended school with the sons of the local gentry,he must have realised the great advantages that they enjoyed, not through talent but by birth. They could move more freely around the country and get permission from the Queen to go abroad. They were also the group from which leaders were drawn, expecting others to listen to them and do what they said. It was also a time of increasing rural poverty as poor harvests forced up the price of corn while wages fell. Many rural families were forced into begging for the food they could no longer afford to buy. Bands of destitute men, women and children roamed the countryside searching for food and work. Those who owned land and controlled Parliament passed savage laws to prevent beggars from wandering away from their home areas   Men were hanged just because they had no way of supporting themselves.

Tudor woodcuts of beggars and 'masterless men'

For the next ten years of his life, John set out to turn himself from a country nobody into a skilled and battle-hardened soldier, with at least the outward signs of a gentleman. He needed enough money to avoid having to earn his living by his own labour, a coat of arms, and a recognised title. He took the first step by doing what many young men do when they come from poor areas with little prospect of getting a good job even today. He joined the Army.

Fighting the Spanish

England was still at war with Spain. Queen Elizabeth had sent Peregrine Bertie, Lord Willoughby, the landlord of the Smith's farm, to command her army in the 'Low Countries', what we now call Holland and the Flanders part of Belgium They were fighting in support of the Protestant Dutch who had rebelled against the Spanish armies occupying their land. In England, they sang this drinking song, to celebrate Lord Willoughby's courage and an English victory, much as we sing football songs today.

My Lord Willoughbies Welcome Home
(to the tune 'Lord Willoughby')

The fifteenth day of July, with glist'ning speare and shield,
A famous fight in Flanders was foughten in the field:
The most courageous officers were the English Captains three,
But the bravest in the Battel was brave Lord Willoughby.

'Stand to it, noble pikemen and look you round about;
And shoot you right, you bow-men, and we will keep them out;
You musquet and calliver men, do you prove true to me,
I'll be the foremost man in fight,' says brave Lord Willoughby.

The English 'fought it out most furiously' for seven long hours, until the Spanish were defeated by one last charge, led of course by 'the brave Lord Willoughby'. Perhaps John Smith heard the song in the ale-houses around Louth and Alford where Lord Willoughby was a local hero.

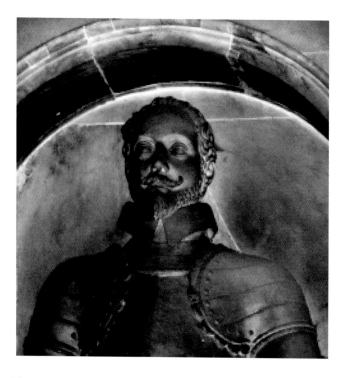

The tomb of Sir Peregrine Bertie, the 'brave Lord Willoughby'
in Spilsby Parish Church

Thousands of young Englishmen went to learn the life of a soldier in the bloody battles just across the North Sea. Elizabeth had no English standing army, so troops were raised locally and young men learnt to fight and survive as best they could. John Smith was about seventeen when he left Willoughby to serve under Captain Joseph Duxbury in this campaign, learning to ride a horse and use his weapons. He must have been a good enough soldier to come home alive when so many died.

Servant to the Berties

When John got back to Lincolnshire, Lord Willoughby chose him to accompany his younger son to France to visit his older brother. They planned to travel together in Europe, the sort of tour which rich young English gentlemen enjoyed. The party had permission from the Queen to be away for three years, travelling with a tutor and two servants, one of whom was to be John. So the young soldier went off to the Willoughby's home at Grimsthorpe Castle in June 1599. They travelled all over France, but it was not long before the brothers decided that they had no further use for John Smith and sent him home. It is easy to imagine that the young soldier must have found carrying the luggage and grooming the horses very dull after fighting in a war. He probably annoyed the two young gentlemen as much as he was to annoy those who considered themselves better than him at every stage in his life.

John Smith as
a young
soldier
by Abbie J.

On his way home, John met a Scotsman who gave him letters to take to the court of King James VI, an opportunity too good to miss for an ambitious young man keen to better himself. He found a ship sailing to Leith near Edinburgh. But the ship was wrecked on Holy Island, off the Northumberland coast. John survived this adventure and took his letters to Edinburgh, but the Scots were not impressed. Smith had neither the money nor the position to become a courtier. Disappointed and frustrated, he had to return to Willoughby.

Knight in armour

Travelling with the Bertie brothers had given him a taste for the life of a gentleman. He wanted to be like them, to be accepted as a member of a privileged class. Back at Willoughby, he was still just a farmer's son, so he arranged for his brother to run the farm and planned his transformation into a 'knight in armour'. He started in a wood, not far from Willoughby, taking with him a good horse from the farm, some old armour, and a lance and ring to practice fighting on horse-back, or 'tilting' as it was called. He even took a boy from the village to be his page. Living rough in the woods, he studied two books, 'Machiavelli's Art of War' and what he called 'Marcus Aurelius', a text on how to be a leader.

Smith stayed in the woods, galloping up and down the paths, practising his riding, for much of the summer. He and his page lived in a shelter of boughs, poaching deer for the pot. Somehow, word of this strange training camp reached the ears of a very famous horseman, none other than Theodora Polaloga, the riding master employed by Lord Clinton at Tattershall Castle. Polaloga sent a message to John, offering him riding lessons, possibly at Lord Willoughby's suggestion. For John, it must have been a bit like being offered driving lessons by Michael Schumacher! He joined the household at Tattershall, and learnt how to fight as gentlemen fought, on horseback with lance, sword and pistol, in the castle tiltyard. He also had the chance to learn some Italian and other European languages.

'Galloping up and down the paths on a farm horse with borrowed armour' by Dean

Tattershall Castle

Once he had mastered the skills of combat and had read his books on how to lead men and win wars, he was impatient to put his skills to use. He had no wish to go back to the mud of the Low Countries and the fighting between the Christian armies of the English and the Spanish. So he decided to find adventure in a very different war in which Christian armies in southern and eastern Europe were desperately resisting Turkish armies invading Europe.

He made his way across Europe, no doubt helped by his Latin, the common language of all educated men. All the beatings at Alford and Louth Grammar Schools must have seemed worthwhile. His journey took him through France, down to the Mediterranean sea. He joined a ship full of Catholic sailors who discovered that he was a Protestant and promptly threw him overboard. Picked up by a more friendly crew, he helped them to capture a Venetian ship which they shared as a prize. Smith reached Italy, with a bag of money and a valuable box. He was now enjoying his own Grand Tour of Europe that any young gentleman would have been pleased to undertake. Eventually, he reached Vienna in Austria and joined the Christian army, fighting to stop the Turks from getting any further into Europe.

Fighting the Turks

Smith soon saw action. His unit was sent to help a city surrounded by the Turkish army. Smith managed to get a message to the besieged forces in the town by using coded signal fires. His message told the defenders that an attack would come from one direction. The Turks were convinced that the attack would come from the other. When the Turks turned to defend themselves against this phantom army, the Christians in the town and their army outside, joined forces and routed the Turks. After this success, Smith was made an officer in the army with the rank of Captain and given a cash reward. Plain John Smith, the tenant farmer's son, now had a title and some money but he still lacked a coat of arms.

Part of the Travels of Capt: IOHN SMITH a mongst TVRKES. TARTARS and others. extracted out of the HISTORY by IOHN PAY. How hee releeued OLVMPAGH by a stratagem of Lights Chap 6

He had read about the use of fireworks in war in one of his books. The Christian army was trying to capture a town held by the Turks. Smith had earthenware pots filled with gunpowder, tar and musket balls. He attached a burning fuse and sent these 'fiery dragons' flying through the air into the town. When his fire-bombs exploded, many Turks were slaughtered and the city captured.

Smith was then involved in another attack on a city held by the Turks. Progress was slow and the defenders taunted the Christian army outside their gates with a challenge. If the Christians would put forward a champion to fight their Lord Turbashaw to the death, they would accept the result. It was like David and Goliath. John Smith volunteered to be the Christian champion. He rode out in front of the two armies, in full armour and carrying his lance. He was confident that the skills which Polaloga had taught him at Tattershall would stand him in good stead. When the two champions charged at each other, Smith's lance went through the slit in the Turk's helmet and killed him. He cut off Turbashaw's head and presented it to his general. A second Turk, Grualgo, now stepped forward to challenge Smith. He too lost his life, his head and his armour. Smith now challenged the Turks to send out a third champion if any dare. Bonny Mulgro rode forward, and exchanged pistol shots with Smith. Both missed, so it was battle axes next. Mulgro's great blow nearly killed Smith but his skill as a horseman saved him and he killed the third Turk with a dagger in the back.

Smith was now a hero. He was given a fine horse, a Turkish sword, and a belt worth a lot of money. Encouraged by Smith's triumph, the Christian army redoubled their efforts and captured the town. Smith's real reward came from the Christian commander. He gave him the right to have a coat of arms on his shield. This badge of three Turks heads and the Latin motto 'Vincere est vivere', 'to conquer is to live', could now be displayed. All could see that Smith had become a gentleman. He was also given a pension of three hundred gold coins a year for life. John Smith of Willoughby was now 'Captain John Smith', complete with a coat of arms and enough money not to have to work for his living.

John Smith's Coat
of Arms by Abbie J

His Combat with GRVALGO. Capt of three hundred horsmen.
Chap. 7

How he slew BONNY:MVLGRO. Chap. 7.

Illustrations from John Smith's 'True Travels' (1630)

His success was not to last. The Christian army of thirteen thousand was attacked by an enemy army of forty thousand. Thousands of soldiers from both sides were left dead or wounded on the battlefield. One of them was Smith. Fortunately, his fine suit of armour showed the victors that he was probably more valuable alive than dead, to be ransomed for money or sold off as a captive. So they stripped him of all his armour and took him to a slave market. With other survivors from the Christian Army, Smith was marched off in a gang chained at the neck, to Constantinople, the Turkish capital city, and sold into slavery.

Smith was lucky again. A young Turkish noblewoman, called Charatza Tragabigzanda, the girl from Trebizond, bought him, to work in her household. She soon discovered that although he was English, they both knew some Italian. But before his relatively comfortable life could develop into a friendship, his mistress sent him away again.

Murdered with a flail

'John Smith was sent to the brother of the girl from Trebizond, hoping to be treated well, given clean clothes and taking his meals with his master. But he was treated as a slave, doing all the hard jobs and chores that no-one else wanted to do. The master made him work in the corn field day after day, sorting the straw from the corn, with a flail. When his master demanded that John worked faster to get the field done, John was angry and swung round with the flail. In a flash his master's body was on the ground. John hit his master's head, killing him and putting on his clothes. He rode off on his master's horse, to escape but he was still wearing an iron collar to show that he was a slave. He travelled on, hoping that he would not be a slave again, trying to find someone who could take off his iron collar.'
(Katrina C)

From John Smith's 'True Travels' (1630)

For sixteen days, he galloped north, until he reached an outpost of the Russian Empire on the River Don. The governor there took pity on him, struck off his iron collar and sent him on his way back to the west. Smith managed to find his former commander who gave him the money he was owed and a written certificate of the award of his coat of arms. As he travelled to England, he kept his money and his document safe, getting back to London in the last months of 1604. Thanks to his own efforts and his extraordinary ability to survive, he could now tell everyone about his coat of arms, his money and his record as a soldier. But without the help of Sir Peregrine Bertie, and his sons, he might still have been just the farmer's son from Willoughby.

A new king

Sailing up the Thames past the Tower to the City of London, the twenty four year old soldier must have wondered what further adventures life had in store for him. Smith had left England in the last years of Queen Elizabeth's life, with her armies still fighting the Spanish. There were still no English possessions on the coast of America to rival the huge territories controlled by the Spanish.

He returned to find King James I (King James VI of Scotland) on the throne, surrounded by Scottish favourites. The King spoke with a very strong Scottish accent and slurred his speech so it was difficult for the English to understand him. He was so afraid of water that he seldom washed and as he tended to spill his food down the front of his doublet, he must have looked scruffy and smelled strongly!

James I of England and VI of Scotland

James hated disagreements, especially between religious groups. He wanted all his people to be contented members of the Church of England. But those who were Puritans wanted the Church to be free from many of the things that reminded them of the Catholic church. James met them in a conference at Hampton Court in 1604. Although he did agree to a new translation of the Bible, he refused to accept that the Church should be reformed and demanded that the Puritans should obey their Bishops. He threatened to 'harry them out of the land' if they refused to conform to the laws of the Church. The new Bible, which is still called the 'King James Bible', was finished in 1611. Many of the Puritan clergy refused to conform and were deprived of their livings as ministers of the Church. Some decided that they would have to leave England.

The English Catholics had even higher hopes. Ever since the reign of Queen Elizabeth, they had been forced to attend Protestant services in the Church of England and punished for holding their own services. They hoped that James would change the law, as he was married to a Catholic queen. But James disappointed them as well and the anti-Catholic laws stayed in place. Frustrated Catholics began to plot together to bring down the King. They planned to blow up the whole Parliament building, with all the Royal Family. This Gunpowder Plot failed when a Catholic soldier, Guy Fawkes, was caught in the cellars under the Houses of Parliament. He was preparing to set light to a huge stack of gunpowder on November 5th 1605, an event which we still celebrate on Guy Fawkes' Night every year.

James also tried to avoid unnecessary wars. He quickly agreed a peace with Spain and sent no more armies to support the Protestant rebels in the Low Countries. He encouraged English sailors to explore the world beyond Europe, and agreed to the development of companies based in London to trade with the East Indies and with Russia. Very rich men like Raleigh were no longer prepared to risk their money on sending settlers to new colonies, and James agreed that a Company should be set up with the specific purpose of establishing a colony in Virginia as a business venture. Anyone could buy shares in this plan, and the list of investors included towns, City Companies and the leading citizens of England, from the Archbishop of Canterbury (£75), to Robert Cecil, Earl of Shrewsbury (£333 6s 8d). Included in the Company list of subscribers was a much more modest investor, Captain John Smith (£9). He was attracted no doubt by the Company's promotion of the rich profits that they were sure to make as soon as the colony was established.

The English knew that in Central America, the land formed a narrow barrier between the Atlantic and the Pacific. They thought that settlers in Virginia would also find a way through the new continent, by sailing up the wide rivers that earlier explorers had found in the part of Virginia known as the Chesapeake. Once through, they would be able to reach the rich trade in spices and silks from China and India. As a third and much less important aim, they also planned to take the faith of the Church of England to the Native American people of Virginia, already called 'Indians' or, more often, 'savages'.

'Plentiful gold...'

The Company promoted the idea that Virginia was full of gold to encourage men to join the venture, but this rosy view was already being scoffed at. In 1605, a play on the London stage, 'Eastward Ho', had a scene in which a sea captain was trying to persuade his listeners that Virginia was a wonderful place, already full of Englishmen, who were loved by the Indians who brought them unimaginable treasure. *'Gold is more plentiful there than copper is with us.....all their cooking pans and chamber pots are pure gold...and, as for rubies and diamonds, they go and gather them on the seashore'.* In the play, the gullible would-be colonists set off from London on their voyage to Virginia, only to be wrecked on the Isle of Dogs, just down the Thames!

The leaders of the Virginia Company recruited men to lead the expedition, some of whom had already sailed across the Atlantic to the American shore. While they were at sea, the overall commander, or 'Admiral', was to be Captain Christopher Newport. He was an expert privateer, probably the most successful raider on Spanish shipping of his day.

He had lost an arm fighting the Spanish and was forty seven when they sailed. Captain Bartholemew Gosnald, Newport's deputy, was a very different man. Educated at Cambridge University, he had been a successful lawyer before he too turned to privateering and exploring the Atlantic. In 1602, he reached what we now call New England and sailed north along the coast, mapping and naming places like Cape Cod and the island still called Martha's Vineyard after his baby daughter. When he returned to London, he was keen to join the Virginia venture, together with his brother and cousin. Many of the others who went were recruited through Gosnald, from his home county of Suffolk. It is likely that Gosnald met John Smith in London. Listening to Smith's stories of travel and adventure, Gosnald may have decided that the young soldier would be a useful man to take.

The arms of the Virginia Company, from the window of Willoughby Church

Most of those who invested their money in the Virginia Company stayed safely in London. Some did join the venture, prepared to risk both their money and their lives. Many had the status of 'gentleman', but little hope of becoming rich unless they found gold in Virginia. George Percy, the younger brother of the Earl of Northumberland, one of the richest men in England, knew he would not inherit his brother's title or his wealth. So he risked his life and a £20 investment in the Virginia adventure.

Many of the men who were recruited were very poor, with hard lives in the stinking backstreets of London. They knew that they were risking their lives, but could only get to Virginia by agreeing to work for the Company as servants and labourers. The Company agreed to support them with food and shelter for all the time that they worked. If they survived these years of service, they would be given a grant of land in Virginia to develop for themselves.

The stinking streets of London from a Tudor woodcut

Going to Virginia

Families think nothing of going to America today for a holiday and it takes no more than a few hours to get there.

'I went with my mum, my dad, my brother and another family on a plane for eight hours for a holiday to Florida. It was a long journey but we still managed to occupy ourselves. The other family weren't sat near us but we kept going to see them. When we finally got off the plane we drove to the hotel to find that the lady had given the room to someone else. My dad was appalled! The lady rang up another hotel manager and she let us stay there. We drove up to the hotel, unpacked our cases from the car, went to our room. Then we all went to a restaurant for tea and back to the hotel to sleep. We were very tired.

In the morning we went for some breakfast and then went to the supermarket to get some food for the villa we were going to be moved into. The villa was huge and had a swimming pool in a big conservatory. It was great because we went to a different Disneyland Park every other day. The days that we did not go to a park we just stayed at the villa relaxing and going in the swimming pool. Also we went shopping for clothes and toys. It was a fantastic holiday and even after two weeks we never wanted to leave, but we had to. (Georgina M.)

It was already mid-December in 1606, when one hundred and five men and boys boarded three ships, the Susan Constant, the Godspeed and the Discovery, moored at Blackwall Steps on the River Thames. It is hard to imagine just how small and uncomfortable these ships must have been. They were cargo vessels, with a cabin for the captain but no other accommodation. Each of the settlers and the crews who sailed the ships had little more than deck-space and a beam from which to hang a hammock. The largest, the Susan Constant was about 82 feet long and 25 feet wide, not much bigger than a cricket pitch. She carried a total of 71 men including the crew. The smallest, the Discovery, was half the size, with 20 men on board. Set alongside the modern Queen Mary II transatlantic liner over 1000ft long, they would have been like a row of ducklings bobbing along in her wake!

Crammed with the men into the ships were all the supplies of food for the voyage and for the first few months in Virginia. They took swords and muskets, trading goods such as beads and copper to tempt the Indians, all their personal belongings and even the parts of a smaller boat to assemble when they reached Virginia. Barrels of beer, enough to last them all the way to America, were stored in the hold.

Stuck in the Channel

Just before Christmas, they sailed on the prevailing SW wind down the Thames. When they had to turn south and west into the mouth of the Channel, the square-rigged ships could make no headway. For almost a month, in mid-winter, the three ships rode at anchor in a rough sea just off the east coast of Kent. Passengers and crew suffered and quarrelled, sea-sick and cold. Their Chaplain, Rev. Robert Hunt, was so ill that the others thought that he would die but he insisted on staying on board, in spite of the fact that his home on land was no more than ten miles away.

Eventually, the wind changed to the east and the ships could sail down the Channel and out into the Atlantic ocean. They followed the long route, 'south until the butter melts and then west'. The Trade Winds carried them over three thousand miles across the Atlantic to the islands of the West Indies. Captain John Smith was a passenger on the Susan Constant and soon got into an argument with the gentlemen on board who could not stand his know-all attitude. They accused him of mutiny, so Captain Newport had him imprisoned on board the ship for the rest of the voyage.

They reached the West Indies by late March and began to island-hop north and west through the waters of the Caribbean. With good weather, plentiful food and friendly trading with the people of the Islands, the voyage went well. But they still could not get on with John Smith. At the Island of Nevis, they were so fed up with him that they actually built a gallows, intending to hang him. But, according to his own account, Smith 'could not be persuaded to mount the gallows'.

From the West Indies, Newport sailed north out of sight of land for ten days. The crews of the three ships thought that they had gone past their destination, when a powerful storm pushed them in towards the American coast and they discovered that they were at the mouth of a great bay. They had found the Chesapeake.

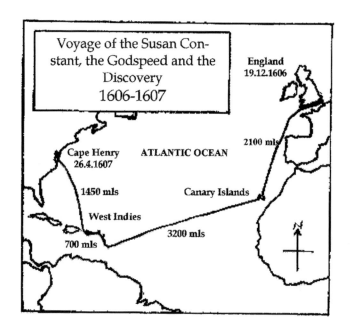

Voyage of the Susan Constant, the Godspeed and the Discovery 1606-1607

England
19.12.1606

Cape Henry
26.4.1607

ATLANTIC OCEAN

2100 mls

1450 mls

Canary Islands

West Indies

3200 mls

700 mls

N

After four months of terrible discomfort on board the three tiny ships, a small party of gentlemen went ashore on the southern point. They named it Cape Henry in honour of the Prince of Wales, King James' eldest son. John Smith was left on board the Susan Constant, still a prisoner.

First landing

Cape Henry's sandy shore seemed deserted to the small group of Englishmen, who first walked across the beach and into the dunes on the 26th April, 1607. They found 'fair meadows and goodly tall trees' but little else. But others had seen them. Soon Indian arrows had wounded two of the English. They hurried back to their ships to complete an important task.

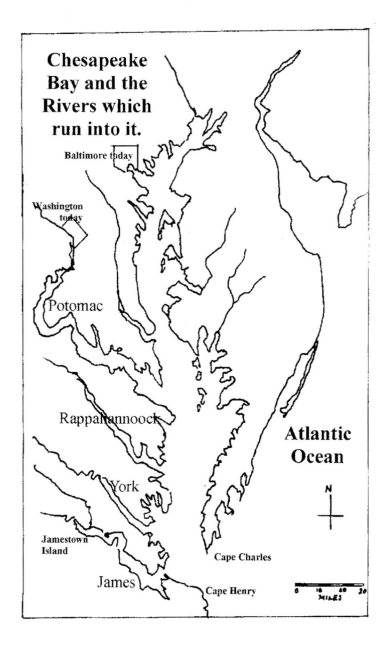

Chesapeake Bay and the Rivers which run into it.

Baltimore today

Washington today

Potomac

Rappahannoock

York

Jamestown Island

James

Cape Charles

Cape Henry

Atlantic Ocean

N

MILES

The leaders of the Virginia Company in London had given each ship a box of instructions to be opened within a day of their arrival in Virginia. With these instructions, they would also find the names of those who had been chosen by the Company as the members of the Council. This group of men were to be in charge of the colony once they reached America. So the box was opened and the names read out.

Six were predictable. Captain Newport, the commander of the Susan Constant, Captain Gosnald of the Godspeed, and Captain Radcliffe of the Discovery, were the first three. They had done well to keep their ships together and bring all their passengers safely to Virginia, except for a gentleman who had died from the heat while foolishly trying to climb a hill in the West Indies. The next three members of the council were rich and influential. Edward Maria Wingfield had invested a lot of his own money in the Company. George Kendall had the support of Robert Cecil, King James' Chief Minister. John Martin was the son of the Lord Mayor of London and had close connections with the City Companies who contributed much of the money for the venture. All six had the rank of gentleman and all were used to being in charge. But the seventh name must have been a shock, Captain John Smith. He was the irritating young soldier and farmer's son who claimed to have a coat of arms and refused to show them the respect that they believed was their right. He was also to be a member of the Council but the other six simply refused to allow him to join them.

'Not to offend the naturals'

The Company's instructions went on to tell them to be 'careful not to offend the naturals'. The advice was good as the settlers would have to depend on trading with the Indians to get enough food to survive until they could grow crops for themselves. They were also told to find a permanent place for their settlement as soon as possible. It had to be well away from the sea where prying Spanish eyes might find them and try to wipe out the colony. As soon as they could, they were to find saleable goods to send home on the Susan Constant and Godspeed to make a profit for the company. The little Discovery was to stay in Virginia so that they could use her to store their weapons and to explore the rivers which ran into Chesapeake Bay.

Whatever else they did, they were to keep the Indians afraid of their guns and to make sure that no-one who could stop them getting back to their ship was allowed to live between their settlement and the shore. Lastly, no-one was allowed to go back to England without permission or to write home with discouraging messages about life in Virginia. The Company wanted nothing but good news to reach England.

Having put up a cross at Cape Henry to give thanks to God for their safe passage from England, they spent the next few days putting together the boat they had brought with them and exploring the mouth of the Chesapeake and the lower parts of the river they called the James. They landed at one point near to an Indian village and were welcomed by the 'naturals'. They shared their meal and were entertained with dancing and treated as honoured guests. Their Indian hosts were naked apart from leather aprons and armed with bows and arrows. Although a book had been written by one of the Roanoke settlers to provide the English with phrases of the Algonquin language spoken by Indians all down the Virginia coast, no-body had thought to bring a copy with them on their voyage to Virginia. Communication between the English and the Indians had to be in sign language.

Native American house typical of the people living around the
Chesapeake area in the 17th century

Head of a
bald eagle

Early May in the Chesapeake region is one of the best times
of the year. The bright sun lights up the water and the trees
are in full leaf. The bald eagles still nest in the tree-tops and
feed on fish from the wide rivers. It was no wonder that

they thought that they had reached a 'heaven on earth' after four months cooped up in tiny ships on the great ocean.

On May 12th, they stopped at a place which had good soil, and plenty of rabbits and turkeys, good to eat before their crops ripened. They called it Archer's Hope, but Wingfield and Newport preferred another place, a low island on the northern shore of the river. The ships could be brought in close to the shore in deep water for an anchorage. The island was hidden by bends in the river from prying Spanish eyes. It was linked to the mainland by a narrow neck of land which could easily be defended. It seemed a good place although the soil was poor and the land very low-lying. They called it Jamestown Island.

Replicas of the Susan Constant, the Godspeed and the Discovery moored at Jamestown Settlement today

Once the ships were anchored and their tents and provisions brought ashore, the six members of the Council finished what they had been instructed to do by electing the first

President. They elected the rich gentleman, Edward Maria Wingfield. John Smith was still a prisoner and was not consulted. They soon realised that they needed every able-bodied man to help clear the trees to make space for their tents and to make small gardens to plant crops. So Smith was released from his fetters and allowed to work but not to join the Council.

The English were pleased to welcome a visitor to their camp, an Indian Chief, bringing a gift of venison. White tailed deer are still plentiful on Jamestown Island. Pleased that the Indians were so friendly, Wingfield decided that Jamestown would not need proper defences and their guns would stay in store on the Discovery. He did not want 'to offend the naturals'. Although this policy seemed madness to some, including John Smith, the settlement remained defenceless.

Towards the end of May, Captain Newport took John Smith and a party of twenty men, including many of his own sailors, up the River James in the small boat. Smith had collected Algonquin words and was able to make himself understood by the Indians. He asked them where the river led to, and was told of waterfalls and a range of mountains. Beyond the mountains, the Indians told them, the river led to a great sea. Or that was what they thought the Indians said. When they tried to get up the river, the English got little further than the falls.

They also learnt from the Indians of a Great Chief. His name was Powhatan and his empire stretched across all the rivers which ran into the Chesapeake. He controlled the tribes by ruthless cruelty, demanding that they pay him tribute. He had heard a prophecy that a nation would rise out of one part of the Chesapeake who would destroy his empire. Powhatan had the whole population of that area massacred, men, women and children.

While Newport and his party were away exploring, the Indians near Jamestown attacked the settlement with hundreds of warriors. Many of the English were wounded and one was killed. Only when one of the Godspeed's guns was loaded with bar-shot and fired at a tree bringing it crashing to the ground did the terrified Indians run away. Newport realised that the policy of being very friendly to the Indians and leaving the settlement without defences would result in the English being wiped out by the next Indian attack. He ordered that a triangular fort be built, from tree trunks set in the ground. At each corner, they built a platform on which one of the heavy guns from the ships could be mounted.

Rebuilt timber palisade on the site of the fort, Jamestown Island

The settlement could now be defended. The Council met to discuss John Smith's position. President Wingfield put the case for sending him home, as in his view, Smith had caused trouble from the start. Fortunately for Smith, Newport and the Rev Robert Hunt came to his defence and he was at last allowed to take his rightful place as a member of the Council.

Good news from Virginia

After less than two months at Jamestown, Newport sailed back to England on the Susan Constant. He took with him an account of how wonderful Virginia was, how successful they had been and how friendly the Indians were, the message the Virginia Company wanted to hear. The Council censored any letters from the settlers to make sure that no-one spoilt the good news. Newport promised to be back in twenty weeks with more supplies, a hollow promise as it had taken him eighteen weeks to sail out to Virginia.

Once Newport's hard-working sailors had gone, progress on developing the settlement ground to a halt. Those who were gentlemen were unwilling to soil their hands with manual labour and those who were more used to work saw little point in making an effort while they could draw rations from the common store. But the stock of food they had brought with them was rapidly being used up and the beer that they had to drink on board ship had long since run out. Soon, each man had to survive on a daily ration of boiled barley and boiled wheat, and even that was beginning to rot. The flow of the river from which they drank slowed down in the summer heat and became more and more muddy and salty. They still drank it, as no-one had the energy or inclination to dig a well. The whole settlement seemed resigned to sitting in their tents on a swampy island buzzing with insects in the summer heat until Newport returned.

Swamps on Jamestown Island

Men began to die

As the sun got hotter and the air steamier, men began to die. Some were sick, some starving. By mid-August, almost all those who were still alive were ill, even Smith and Radcliffe. If the Indians had attacked then, they could have over-run the fort as only five men were still strong enough to defend it. Amongst the dead was Captain Bartholemew Gosnald. They buried him with his captain's staff and fired a musket volley salute over his grave. Almost half of the settlement died that first summer. Whether it was typhus spread by lice from man to man or typhoid fever and dysentery, spread through the foul water that they drank, men still died. The colony seemed doomed.

One man seemed to stay fit and well. President Edward Wingfield never seemed to be hungry. Smith accused him of keeping food for himself while others starved. The Council members decided that Wingfield should be deposed and Radcliffe elected President in his place. When Wingfield was put on trial for his selfishness, he claimed to have had nothing extra apart from a little salad oil, but the others knew that he had been secretly eating beef and eggs, oatmeal and wine from a private store. He was convicted and Smith decided to remind them all that Wingfield had accused him of mutiny on the voyage out. A jury of settlers decided that Smith was not guilty of this charge and awarded him £200 damages to be paid by Wingfield. All Wingfield's private stores were handed over to Smith, who gave them to the common store for everyone to enjoy.

Recognising that Smith had energy and ability, President Radcliffe decided to make him supply officer for the settlement in charge of getting supplies by trading with the Indians and building houses. Smith must have used the skills he learnt at home in Willoughby as the first houses built in Jamestown were mud and stud, just like the simple houses of East Lindsey back home.

Trading for food

Smith also realised that the settlement needed supplies of food from trading with the Indians to replenish their stores. While most of the colonists continued to do little but wait for Newport to return, Smith left Jamestown with a small group to explore the rivers and find Indians willing to trade. He knew that he would only be successful if the Indians believed that the English were still strong and were afraid of the English guns. This trading for corn kept the settlement going through the autumn months until the coming of winter brought a plentiful supply of food from the flocks of duck and snow geese flying down from the north.

In December 1607, when Newport's return was long overdue, Smith set out again from Jamestown with nine settlers to explore the rivers to the north. They had travelled fifty miles upstream when Smith went on with three men into the wilderness. The seven left in the boat had strict instructions to stay there. Things went badly wrong when the Indians watching them from the woods used their women to tempt the seven ashore and then attacked them. All but one of the English escaped, but he was caught, tied to a tree and killed very slowly by cutting off his fingers with mussel shells, skinned and then disembowelled. It was an awful warning to the rest of what the 'naturals' would do to any Englishman who fell into their hands.

Smith and his companions were with their Indian guides when they too were surprised by a large number of Indians. Using one of his guides as a human shield, Smith tried to escape, but he fell into a deep bog and had to surrender. The Indians took him to their village where to his surprise he was treated well, and given food and shelter. They clearly wanted to find out as much as they could from him, asking why he had come. Smith tried to persuade them that the English at Jamestown would soon come looking for him and attack their village with guns.

They agreed to let him send a message to Jamestown to tell the settlers there that he was still alive. His written note was taken to Jamestown and warned the English that they should prepare for imminent attack. Smith's message told the Jamestown settlers to fire the cannon to make sure that the Indians were thoroughly frightened, before they were allowed to return to the village with presents. All this was done, and the messengers brought back both the gifts and their amazement that Smith could make a piece of paper speak!

In Powhatan's house

The Indians decided to take their prisoner to Powhatan. He would know what to do with him. John Smith was taken to the Great Chief's village and into Powhatan's hut. In the gloom, he saw an impressive figure, surrounded by his women and warriors. Powhatan was over sixty, but still fit, broad shouldered and every inch the warrior king. Smith was given water to wash and food to eat, and questioned again, by Powhatan himself. Why had the English come? What were their plans? Smith told the Emperor that his 'father', Newport, had sent him to look for one of Newport's men, and to find an inland sea. If Smith did not return, Newport himself with all his guns would come to look for him.

It was an idle threat, as Powhatan had Smith completely in his power. He could chose to execute him at any time, but he also knew that the English with their guns could be useful allies in his wars against the tribes to the west. There was also the prophecy that people would come from the Chesapeake and overthrow his people. Perhaps the English were the ones. Powhatan decided Smith was to die, and he was dragged forward to kneel in front of two large stones. The warriors raised their clubs, ready to beat out his brains.

At this point, a young girl rushed forward. Taking Smith's head in her arms, she told her father that if Smith was to die, so would she. The girl was Pocahontas, Powhatan's favourite twelve year old daughter. For a moment the executioners hesitated, and waited for Powhatan's signal. He maintained his dignity. Rather than ordering his distressed daughter to stand aside, he accepted her plea for Smith's life.

Within the illustration:
King Powhatan comands C. Smith to be flayne, his daughter Pokahontas begs his life, his thankfulnes and how he subiected 39 of their kings, reade y history.

printed by James Reeve

From Smith's 'True Travels' (1630)

The Englishman would be spared. He would be more useful making hatchets for the Great Chief and beads for his daughter. Powhatan declared that he and Smith were now friends. Smith would be treated as his son and given land. After much celebrating, he sent Smith back to Jamestown with the promise from Smith that he would give Powhatan two canons and a grindstone. In early January 1608, Smith got back to the settlement with his Indian guides and showed them two large cannons, telling them to take them back if they could. As the guns weighed thousands of pounds, this was clearly impossible. The two Indians returned to their Emperor with gifts that they could carry and which they could not use against the English.

Having escaped execution by the Indians, Smith now found that he faced death at the hands of his own comrades. Radcliffe had appointed Gabriel Archer as a new member of the Council while Smith was away to make sure that they could out-vote Smith. When he returned, they accused him of being responsible for the deaths of the two men who had been killed by the Indians. This was a ridiculous charge but a court was convened and Smith found guilty. Radcliffe sentenced him to death by hanging in the morning.

Newport returns

In the nick of time, Captain Newport's ship arrived back at Jamestown and Newport took command. Smith was reprieved and released. Sixty new colonists landed with supplies enough for all the settlement. But, soon after they landed, one of the new colonists accidentally set fire to the roof of his shelter and soon the whole settlement was in flames. Most of them lost everything they owned. The common store with all the new supplies was burnt to the ground. There was no alternative but to start all over again, to rebuild Jamestown and start to trade again with the Indians for supplies of food.

Now that Newport was back, Powhatan wanted to meet him, so he and Smith took the Discovery to visit his village. Newport stayed on board while Smith took gifts to Powhatan, including a small white greyhound dog, which delighted the Indian leader. Next day, Newport himself came ashore and met Powhatan with Smith acting as their interpreter. Newport wanted to impress the Emperor with his power and generosity and, against Smith's advice, proceeded to give Powhatan all the other presents he had brought, hoping to trade for corn.

Powhatan was less impressed with these than with the dog and provided very little corn in exchange. Smith knew that the way to get a good deal from the Indians was to get them interested in something and then tell them that they would need to offer a lot of corn to get what they wanted. In full sight of Powhatan, he played with some blue beads. Once the Great Chief was interested, Smith told him that they were rare and very valuable. Powhatan now wanted the beads so much that he agreed to give Smith a large amount of corn in exchange. So the English returned to Jamestown with a good supply of food.

Gold fever

Newport then set about the real purpose of his return to Jamestown. While he was in London, he had told the Virginia Company that he had found gold at Jamestown and even took back samples with him. When these were tested and found to be worthless, Newport claimed that he had made a mistake by bringing the wrong samples home. Now the Company expected results. Newport had to find gold when he returned to the Colony. Soon after he arrived back, he ordered most of the settlers to start a search for gold. They loaded all the promising ore onto Newport's ship to take back to London.

Although it was planting time for the crops the English would need later in the year, the fields were neglected. Precious food supplies were used up as everyone searched for gold. John Smith knew that there was no gold. If there had been, the Indians would have found and used it, much as the Aztecs and Incas had done before the Spanish invaded their lands. Smith knew that, for the Indians, their food was their wealth. The tribes paid tribute to Powhatan in what they could grow or hunt or catch, not what they could dig up from the ground. But no-one listened to Smith and gold-fever gripped the colony.

Statue of Pocahontas on Jamestown Island, supposedly a twelve year old Algonquin girl.

While all this was going on, Pocahontas frequently visited Jamestown, fascinated to know more about the English. She played with the boys in the settlement, turning naked cartwheels with them in uninhibited delight. She taught Smith more of her Algonquin language and learnt some

English from him. She was still only about thirteen, not yet a woman in the eyes of her people.

Just before Newport left for London with his cargo of 'gold ore', Powhatan sent him a present of twenty turkeys, suggesting that Newport might like to give him twenty swords in exchange. Newport foolishly agreed. As soon as Newport had gone, Powhatan tried the same exchange with John Smith, who refused to trade weapons which the Indians could use against the English for turkeys from the woods. Powhatan was angry and told his warriors to steal the weapons whenever they could.

With the ship went Wingfield and Archer, two former members of the Council. They would spread poisonous stories about John Smith once they got back to England. Later that month another ship arrived at Jamestown. It had set out with Newport's ship from London, but been separated and stayed in the West Indies for the winter as supplies of food were plentiful there. With the ship came another sixty men to reinforce the settlement where so many had died, but also more mouths to feed.

Jamestown was steadily losing tools and weapons, stolen by the Indians. Some of them were caught and Smith sent word to Powhatan that either the tools and weapons were returned or the Indians would be hung for stealing. This was, after all, the punishment for stealing in England and English law had been followed in Jamestown. Powhatan suggested instead an exchange of prisoners, as the Indians held two Englishmen captive, but Smith decided that the time had come for a show of strength. The colony would only survive if the Indians believed that the English were strong enough to defeat any attack. Smith gathered together a fighting force and led a punitive expedition against the nearest Indian villages. They burnt their houses and wrecked their canoes. These canoes were the Indians' most valuable possessions, made by the long process of burning out the trunks of trees and used for travel and for fishing. No Indians were killed and none taken prisoner, but the message was clear. It was very dangerous to steal from or attack the English. Powhatan returned the English prisoners and Smith released one of the Indians in exchange.

Burning out a tree-trunk to make a canoe

'To conquer is to live'

Powhatan sent Pocahontas with an Indian called Rawhunt to Jamestown to ask Smith to spare the lives of the remaining prisoners. Smith made a great show of releasing them, claiming that it was only because Pocahontas had persuaded him. For a time, there were no more thefts. The Indians knew that the English were to be feared and Smith knew that a frightened Indian was much more use to the settlement than a dead Indian. But Smith's action was criticised in London as it went against the policy of 'not offending the naturals'. It was easy to think this in the safety of London. In Jamestown, the alternative to making the Indians fear the English was not peace, but war. At any time, the overwhelming numbers of Indians could attack them if they thought the English weak. Smith knew the truth of his own motto, 'to conquer is to live'.

The second ship sailed back to London, carrying some cedar boards, but they were of little value. Much more important for the future of Jamestown was a lighter piece of cargo, the hand-written journal which John Smith had kept from the time they left Blackwall Steps. He sent it in the form of a long letter, which was soon edited in London, cutting out any parts that were critical of the Virginia Company. It was printed as 'a True Relation of such occurrences and accidents of note as hath happened in Virginia,' 'written by Captain Smith, Coronell of the said colony, to a worshipful friend of his in England'. The book was a great success, as it was the first proper account of the beginning of the settlement at Jamestown. The unknown editor, without Smith's permission, added a final positive paragraph to say that they were 'in good health, well contented, free from mutinies, in love with one another and, as we hope in a continual peace with the Indians'. That was the message that the Virginian Company wanted everyone to hear but the truth, back in Jamestown, was very different.

John Smith's 'True Relation', sent home as an unauthorised letter and published with much editing in London in 1608

Stung by a fish

Once the ship had gone, John Smith set out again with a party of settlers to explore the north of the Chesapeake river system. He mapped the rivers and the coast, naming places as they went, reaching the very edge of Powhatan's empire. Smith knew that if he could establish links with Powhatan's enemies, the colony would be more secure as the English could play off one tribe against another.

Sailing back down the great Bay, Smith's boat grounded in the shallows off the mouth of the Rappahannock river. Smith leant over the side of the boat looking for fish for their evening meal and used his sword to spear a shadowy shape in the shallow water. The fish was a stingray. As he hauled it aboard the boat, it wrapped its long tail around his arm and stung him. For a time, Smith thought he was going to die. His arm and side swelled up from the poisonous sting. Groaning in agony, he told the men to take him on shore and dig a grave to bury him. But the doctor with the party used an ointment to treat the arm. Slowly Smith recovered and by evening, he was well enough to enjoy the meal that the fish provided for them all. On their way back to Jamestown, Smith with an injured arm let the local Indians believe that they had been in a fight with the powerful tribes to the north and had defeated them. The Indians spread the story. This man was strong and not to be provoked.

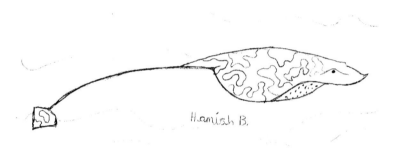

Southern stingray, still found in the Chesapeake

President Smith

Meanwhile, back at Jamestown Island, President Radcliffe was behaving increasingly strangely. He had decided that he needed a palace suitable for his status as President. In the full heat of the summer, all other work was stopped. The men had to fell trees and clear land on this completely unnecessary project. They were hot, ill and angry and, by the time that John Smith returned, keen to get rid of Radcliffe. He was deposed and Smith elected President in his place. He was the only one left of the original council of seven and the only man capable of holding the colony together. On the 8th of September 1608, John Smith of Willoughby finally became the President of Virginia. His term of office was just one year, one year more of the colony's fragile survival.

Shortly afterwards, Captain Newport arrived again at Jamestown, this time with another seventy new colonists, including two women. One of them was unmarried, joining a settlement of about two hundred men. By Christmas, she was married! The Virginia Company, impatient with the lack of profit from Virginia, had given Newport two new tasks. Firstly, he had to find something of real value, no more promises which turned out to be false. He must find a gold-mine or a route to the Pacific or the survivors from the lost colony at Roanoke. Any one of these would please the Company's investors. Secondly, the Great Chief Powhatan was to be crowned by the English, to show that he accepted the authority of the English King.

The Indians had no any idea what the crowning meant. But that did not matter, Powhatan was to be crowned. As Powhatan would not come to Jamestown for this weird ceremony, Newport set out with a large number of men to 'crown' the Emperor. When they met, Powhatan would not kneel for the coronation, so one of the English leant on his shoulder. Newport popped the crown on his head and the English fired their guns in celebration. Powhatan was startled but remained dignified. In response to the King of England's gift of a crown, he gave Captain Newport his deerskin cape embroidered with cowrie shells and his old leather shoes. The cape and shoes are still in a museum in Oxford. The crown soon disappeared.

'Powhatan's cape', from the Ashmolean Museum in Oxford

John Smith was now in charge of the Colony and helped set up small factories to make glass and pitch which could be sent back to England when Newport sailed away. With the ship, Smith also sent a bitter letter to the Virginia Company. He complained that what they really needed in Virginia was not more gentlemen, or experts in testing for gold and workers in glass, but hard-working farmers, fishermen, carpenters and stone-masons. They needed men prepared to use their sweat and their skill to build a community which could sustain itself. Only then would the colony generate the trade which the Company had hoped for.

With the ship gone, Smith tried to make the colony run more effectively. He knew that they had neglected the essential work of planting crops so that the English were still totally dependant on the Indians for food. He persuaded the settlers, even the gentlemen, to clear more land by cutting down trees, work which to their great surprise, they actually enjoyed.

Virginia in the Fall

But as the colours of autumn turned to winter, the need to get food from the Indians became urgent again. Friendly trading was no longer possible. The Indians would only provide corn for Jamestown if they were afraid. Smith got some from the neighbouring tribe by reminding them of the threats he had used in the spring and their promise to share their harvest. But it was not enough. The only other source was the great store that Powhatan kept in his own village and Smith decided to try to persuade Powhatan to part with some of it. He led his men to the village and told the great chief what they wanted.

'Lay down your arms' Powhatan suggested, 'and you will be able to load the corn into your boats'. But Smith knew that putting down their weapons would mean certain death. The English kept their pistols loaded and made the Indians carry the corn on to the boats. But by that time, the tidal river had fallen and the boats were stuck on the mud. They would have to stay the night in the village. In the darkness, they had a visitor. It was Pocahontas, come to warn them that they were about to be attacked and urging them to escape. For the second time, she saved Smith's life, knowing that if Powhatan found out, she too would die. Smith and his men slipped out of the village, waited by their boats for the tide to rise and left for Jamestown.

No work, no food

The supply of food should have been enough to last them through to the next harvest, but the settlement at Jamestown was still in chaos. The English were again falling sick from bad water and the Indians were still stealing tools and weapons. Smith called the settlers together and told them what they had to do. The new rule was biblical in its simplicity. *'He that will not work shall not eat'*. This stirred the settlers to action. Within three months, new houses had been built, a well dug for fresh water and forty acres of Indian corn had been planted. A permanent guard was posted on the narrow neck of land where the island joined the mainland to stop anyone running off with tools and weapons.

But just as one crisis had passed, another hit them. The English had brought rats with them in their ships, and the rats were destroying their stores of corn. By early summer, the food was running out again. John Smith decided that the only way that they could survive was to do what the Indians did in time of famine, split into smaller groups and live off the land. Each group was sent to a place where they could survive on what they could collect or catch. Some went down-river to live on oysters which were plentiful on the shore. Others went upstream to live on the fish that came up the river to spawn. Another group even went to live with the more friendly Indians in their village. The policy worked. None of the small groups were attacked and all the English survived.

Young White Tailed deer plentiful in the Chesapeake region

Meanwhile, in London, the Virginia Company had received John Smith's letter but were not pleased with his complaints. They were hardly likely to listen, when all the former leaders of the Colony were in London, each with his complaint about Smith. The Company leaders decided that the time had come either to abandon the Jamestown project or to re-establish it on a much larger scale. This they agreed to do, raising very large sums of money by selling new shares to fund a much larger expedition. Over six hundred individuals risked their money and fifty six of the London City Companies bought shares.

It was enough to start again. Hundreds of volunteers were recruited to go to Jamestown, risking their lives in the new venture on the same indentures that those who had set out in 1607 had accepted. Each was to serve for seven years and then to have the chance of owning and working their own land. A new Royal Charter was signed by King James, giving authority to a single Governor, to replace the system of a Council and an elected President. They decided that the new Governor would not be Captain John Smith. There had been far too many complaints about his autocratic attitude, his dealings with the Indians and his impatience with those who believed themselves to be his betters. Lord De La Warr was made Lord Governor, with Sir Thomas Gates as Lieutenant and Sir George Somers as Admiral. In Virginia, John Smith was still struggling to ensure that there was a Jamestown Colony for them to take over.

Nine ships set out in the new expedition. After a terrible journey right through the heat of a tropical summer in which thirty two would-be colonists died including two babies born at sea, four of the ships reached Jamestown. But none of the appointed leaders were on these ships, neither was a copy of the new Charter. So when they arrived, John Smith challenged the authority of those who led them. Until the new Charter and the Lord Governor arrived, he would remain in charge of Jamestown Settlement and the new arrivals until the end of his term of office as President. He knew that he would eventually have to relinquish the leadership, and also knew that the Company planned to put him in charge of a small settlement at Cape Henry.

But as the summer wore on, the need to ensure that the new settlers survived led to his order to them to join the scattered groups. They were to establish defensible positions and trade with the Indians for food as best they could. This arrangement soon broke down as the new settlers attacked the Indian communities, not trading but killing, men, women and children. John Smith found that he had no effective control over them and, in despair, decided to return to Jamestown to await the arrival of the rest of the fleet.

Terrible burns

As they sailed down the James River, with Smith still President of Virginia, sleeping in the bottom of the boat, a spark from a tobacco pipe, or from the burning end of a musket fuse, landed on the pouch of gunpowder lying in his lap. It exploded, causing a terrible wound. On fire and in agony, Smith jumped overboard only to be pulled out again by the others in the boat. They took their badly wounded President back to Jamestown but there was no proper doctor there to help him. He did not expect to live and in his fever dreamt that a man came into his house to shoot him.

But John Smith survived, although he knew that he could no longer stay in the Jamestown Colony. In early September, as his term of office as President ran out, still unable to walk, he got a passage on one of the ships returning to England. The sailing was delayed while those who wanted to add their complaints about him wrote letters to London. He was falsely accused of many things, including planning to marry the Princess Pocahontas and to make himself Emperor. As his ship sailed away, Pocahontas was told that her friend had died. It was a sad end to the efforts of the one man who had ensured that the colony survived through all the crises of the first two years.

His great achievement is recognised by the modern statue on Jamestown Island. Captain John Smith stands, confident and composed, gazing down the James River to the mouth of Chesapeake Bay and the Atlantic Ocean.

Monument to Captain John Smith on the shore of Jamestown Island near the site of the first settlement

Postscript

If you want to know what happened to John Smith, and to Pocahontas, the Indian Princess who twice saved his life, read the two sequels to this book, *'Mrs John Rolfe, better known as Pocahontas'* and *'Admiral of New England'*. After 1609, when John Smith came home, Jamestown Colony survived, as the first permanent English speaking colony in North America. Thirteen years after Jamestown was first established, the Pilgrim Fathers landed at Plymouth near Cape Cod and established their settlement. Ten years after that, the Massachusetts Bay Company settled the area to the north of Plymouth and founded the large colony which grew into the City of Boston, Massachusetts. Not long after Plymouth, the Catholics established their first settlements in Maryland. All these developments in early American history have their roots in the rich soil of Eastern England, but the first was Jamestown. In 2007, the 400th anniversary of the founding of America will be celebrated in Virginia and in England.

Captain John Smith – outline chronology

1492	Columbus 'discovers' the New World
1509	Henry VIII becomes king
1536	Lincolnshire Rising
1547	Edward VI becomes king
1553	Mary becomes queen
1558	Elizabeth I becomes Queen
1564	William Shakespeare born
1580	John Smith baptized on 9th January
1588	Defeat of the Spanish Armada
1595?	Pocahontas born; Smith works for merchant in Lynn
1596	Smith's father dies
1600?	Smith goes off to fight the Turks
1603	James VI of Scotland succeeds Elizabeth as James I of England
1604	Smith is back in London
1605	Gunpowder Plot fails
1606	First Virginia Company Charter; December, three ships sail for Virginia
1606	Ships arrive in Virginia; Jamestown Colony settled
1608	Smith elected President of Virginia
1609	Smith has to return to England
1614	Pocahontas marries John Rolfe
1617	Pocahontas dies at Gravesend
1620	Pilgrim Fathers settle at Plymouth
1625	Charles I becomes king
1630	Boston, Massachusetts, founded
1631	John Smith dies in London
1649	Charles I executed

Sources

We used the following sources to research this book

Arber, Edward Ed.
   'Captain John Smith Complete Works'
      Birmingham. 1884
Barbour, Philip
   'Pocahontas and her World'
      Robert Hale 1969
   'The Three Worlds of Captain John Smith'. Houghton
      Miflin. 1964
Doherty, Kieron
   'To Conquer is to live'
      Twenty-first Century 2001 *
Hume, Ivor Noel
   'The Virginia Adventure'.
      Knopf. 1994
Kelso, William and Beverley Straube
   'Jamestown Rediscovery 1994-2004'
      APVA 2004
Lemay, J A Leo
   'The American Dream of Captain John Smith'
      UPV. 1991
Mello, Tara Baukus
   'John Smith'
      Chelsea House 2000*
Parker, Michael St John
   'William Shakespeare'.
      Pitkin.2000
Price, David A
   'Love and Hate in Jamestown'
      Knopf. 2003

Shakespeare, William
> *The Complete Works*
>> Ed. Peter Alexander. Collins. 1951

Smith, Bradford
> *'Captain John Smith'*
>> Lipincott. 1953

Wright Hale, Edward
> *'Jamestown Narratives'*.
>> Roundhouse. 1998

 Zucker Stanley, Melanie
> *'John Smith'*
>> Foxhound 2000*

* books written for young people

and the following websites:

Jamestown-Yorktown Foundation at
www.jamestown2007.org/ and at
www.historyisfun.org/jamestown/jamestown.cfm

'Historic Jamestowne' at
www.historicjamestowne.org/index/php

Association for the Preservation of Virginian Antiquities at www.apva.org.

Virtual Jamestown Project at
www.virtualjamestown.org/

Thanks

Many individuals have helped us with this book and we would like to thank them all.

In Lincolnshire, UK:
Sue Belton with the Staff and Governors of St Helena's CE Primary School, Willoughby; Trish Glazier with the Staff and Governors of Partney CE VA Primary School; The Right Hon. The Baroness Willoughby De Eresby; Rev. Daffyd Robinson, Rector of Willoughby; Rev. Richard Ireson, Rector of Alford; Brian Weaver and Eileen Sharpe of St Wilfrid's Church, Alford; Canon Stephen Holdaway, Rector of Louth; James Wheeldon, Robert O'Farrell and Carole Ashcroft of King Edward VI Grammar School, Louth; David Robinson OBE of Louth, Jean Howard, Lincolnshire Blue Badge Guide; Alison McDonald and Simone Pitzal of East Lindsey District Council; the Members of Willoughby Village History Group; Caron Emonton and Shelley Garland of the National Trust; Molly Burkett and Jayne Thompson of Barny Books, Geof Allinson of Allinson and Wilcox;

And in Virginia, USA:
Dr Bill Kelso of the APVA, Jamestown Island; Amy Ritchie of Jamestown 2007; Heather Hower of the Jamestown – Yorktown Foundation; Jeffrey Smith, Karen Thompson, Ed Boyd, Jean Louie and Martha Hanks-Nicholl of the Williamsburg - James City County Public Schools;

And many others who have helped with proof-reading, layout advice, historical information and patience when our interest in American history got in the way of other priorities.